## presents

**BY JOHN KOLVENBACH**

First performed in the UK at the Assembly Rooms
in Edinburgh on 4th August 2006

# Cast

**Ralph**  Mathew Horne
**Manny**  Peter Polycarpou
**Max**  Paul M Meston
**Thomas**  Samuel Roukin

# Creative Team

**Director**  Matt Wilde
**Designer**  Lisa Lillywhite
**Lighting Designer**  Tim Mascall
**Original Music**  Ben Hales
**Casting Director**  Gabrielle Dawes
**Voice and Dialect Coach**  William Conacher
**Company Stage Manager**  Marius Rønning
**Technical Stage Manager**  Anthony Newton
**Sound Designer**  Nick Manning
**Costume Buyer**  Tamsin Rhymes
**Prop Maker**  Aurelie Mann

# For ATC

**Artistic Director**  Gordon Anderson
**Executive Producer**  Emma Dunton
**Administrator**  Kendall O'Neill
**Production Manager**  Simon Sturgess
**Press Agents**  Kim Morgan and Paul Sullivan
**Graphic Design**  Mark Goddard

# Biographies

## Gordon Anderson
### Artistic Director

Gordon is Artistic Director of ATC for whom he has directed *A Brief History of Helen of Troy*, *Jeff Koons*, *Country Music*, *One Minute*, *Out of Our Heads*, *Arabian Night* and *In the Solitude of Cotton Fields*. He has directed three series of *The Catherine Tate Show* for Tiger Aspect/BBC2, as well as directing productions for the Royal Court Theatre, The Bristol Old Vic, the Lyric Hammersmith, the Royal Exchange, English Touring Opera, Scottish Opera and Grange Park Opera. He has also worked with the League of Gentlemen, Mitchell & Webb, Navelgazing and Susan & Janice.

## Emma Dunton
### Executive Producer

Since joining ATC in 2001 Emma has produced *A Brief History of Helen of Troy* by Mark Schultz, *Jeff Koons* by Rainald Goetz, *Country Music* and *One Minute* by Simon Stephens, *Excuses!* by Joan Joel and Jordi Sanchez, *Out of Our Heads* by Susan Earl and Janice Phayre, *Arabian Night* by Roland Schimmelpfennig and *In the Solitude of Cotton-Fields* by Bernard-Marie Koltes. At Volcano Theatre Company she produced and managed the national and international tours of *Macbeth – Director's Cut*, *The Town That Went Mad* and *Private Lives*. Previously she has worked at the British Council and on feature films in Los Angeles.

## Ben Hales  *Composer*

Ben Hales is a musician and songwriter. He has toured extensively with various bands since abandoning a drama degree at Goldsmiths College in 1993. In 2002 he began working as a freelance songwriter and signed to SonyBMG Music Publishing in 2005. He has written songs and performed with numerous artists including Aqualung and Melanie Blatt (All Saints). Production music credits include soundtracks for commercials for Mitsubishi and Wrigley's and original music and sound effects for Splendid Productions' *Resistible Rise of Arturo Ui* and *Animal Farm*. He is currently co-producing Aqualung's third album for Columbia Records.

## Mathew Horne  *Ralph*

Mathew's television credits include writing and performing in *The Catherine Tate Show* (BBC2) and leading roles in *Teachers* (C4) and *20 Things To Do Before You're Thirty* (C4). Guest appearances include *Nathan Barley* (C4), *Carrie & Barrie* (C4), *Doc Martin* (ITV) and *The Smoking Room* (BBC2). Film credits include *Vanity Fair* and short, *Stingray*. His most recent theatre credits include *A Day in the Death of Joe Egg* and *Blue Remembered Hills*.

## John Kolvenbach  *Playwright*

John is the author of *Love Song*, *on an average day*, *Gizmo Love*, *The Gravity of Means* and the recently completed *Fabuloso*. *Love Song* premiered at Steppenwolf in Chicago in the Spring of 2006, directed by Austin Pendelton. *on an average day* ran at the Comedy Theatre in the West End in 2002, starring Woody Harrelson and Kyle MacLachlan, directed by John Crowley. *Gizmo Love* premiered in Cape Cod in 2004. *The Gravity of Means* premiered in New York at MCC.

## Lisa Lillywhite  *Designer*

Lisa's theatre credits include: *On Tour* (Royal Court Theatre/Liverpool Everyman); *Slowtime* (RNT tour); *Gong Donkeys*, *A Carpet a Pony and a Monkey*, *Got to be Happy*, *Blackbird* (Bush Theatre); *The Lisbon Traviata* (Kings Head); *Tape* (Soho Theatre); *Live from Golgotha*, *PWA: the diaries of Oscar Moore* (Drill Hall); *Modern Love* (Queen Elizabeth Hall); *The Changeling* (Southwark Playhouse); *Young Hamlet* (Young Vic); *Musical Youth* (Birmingham Rep tour).

Design for Television includes: *Smash Hits Pollwinners' Party* (T4); *Princes Trust Urban Music Festival* (T4); *The Dimbleby Lecture* (BBC); *The Kiss Awards* (C4); *Song for Wales* (S4C). Lisa was awarded the Arts Foundation Stage Design Fellowship in 2001.

## Tim Mascall
### Lighting Designer

Recent lighting design credits include (London and West End) *Breakfast With Jonny Wilkinson* (Menier Chocolate Factory) *Lies Have Been Told - An Evening With Robert Maxwell* (Trafalgar Studios) *Behind The Iron Mask* (Duchess Theatre), *The Vagina Monologues* (Wyndhams Theatre), *The Road To Nirvana* (King's Head) *Why The Whales Came* (Comedy Theatre), *Professor Bernhardi* and *Rose Bernd* (Arcola Theatre), *Vote Dizzy* (Soho Theatre), *Filler Up* (Drill Hall), *ZooNation Dance* (Sadlers Wells), *When Harry Met Barry* (workshop production at The Venue) *Passion* (Marie Forbes Dance at The Place Theatre) *Dazed* (Fracture Dance Theatre at The Bloomsbury Theatre).

## Paul M Meston  *Max*

*The Barber Of Seville* (Bristol), *The Beauty Queen Of Leenanne* (York), *The Mayor Of Zalamea* (Liverpool), *Girl On A Sofa* (EIF 2002/Shaubuhne Berlin), Berkoff's *Messiah* (UK & Eastern European Tours), *Grimm Tales & More Grimm Tales* (Young Vic, New Victory NYC & World Festival Tours). TV Includes: *The Bill, Casualty, Hollyoaks, Kavanagh QC*. Film Includes: *Passion In The Desert, Closed Circuit, A New Religion*.

## Anthony Newton
### Technical Stage Manager

Anthony graduated from QMUC, Edinburgh in 2004. Out of University he worked as a Designer for 18 months in an Event Lighting Company before pursuing his career in theatre as a freelance Lighting Designer, Production Manager and Technician. Recent work includes designs for The Southwark Playhouse and Stephen Joseph Youth Theatre and Technical Director of The National Student Drama Festival.

## Kendall O'Neill
### Administrator

Kendall joined ATC in April 2006. Originally from Chicago, Kendall spent the last three years working in theatre in New York. She was the Assistant Director on Mark Schultz's *Everything Will Be Different* at Soho Rep. Kendall has also worked for Manhattan Theatre Club, Williamstown Theatre Festival and The Flea Theatre and is a member of both Waterwell and Prospect Theatre Company. This Autumn Kendall will be Assistant Director on the Gate Theatre's production of *Woyzeck* at St Ann's Warehouse in Brooklyn.

## Peter Polycarpou  *Manny*

Peter's extensive and diverse work includes periods with the RSC, RNT and in the West End. He has recently been in a workshop at The Old Vic with Pedro Almodovar and David Levaux in a stage adaptation of the film *All About My Mother*. On TV he has made appearances in *EastEnders*, *The Bill*, *Holby City*, *Casualty*, *Waking The Dead* and many will remember him as Chris Theodopoulopoudos in the BBC's *Birds Of A Feather*. His film credits include *Evita* starring Madonna, Trevor Nunn's RNT production of *Oklahoma!* starring Hugh Jackman and *De-Lovely* starring Ashley Judd and Kevin Kline. More recently in *I Could Never Be Your Woman* with Michelle Pfeiffer and *Beyond Friendship* with Ian Holm. He also has a Manchester Evening News best actor nomination for his performance as Oscar in *The Odd Couple* at The Library Theatre.

## Marius Rønning
### Company Stage Manager

Marius graduated from RADA in 2001 where he trained as a Stage Manager. Since then he has been working freelance. He has worked for Trestle, Tete a Tete, Royal College of Music, New Kent Opera, English Touring Opera, Wee, Soho Theatre Company, Tamasha, Graeae, The Royal Court and ATC. He worked on the ATC productions: *Excuses!*, *Country Music*, *Jeff Koons* and *A Brief History of Helen of Troy*.

## Samuel Roukin  *Thomas*

Samuel's stage credits include *The Taming of the Screw* (Bristol Old Vic, dir Anne Tipton), *Great Expectations* (RSC, dir Declan Donnellan), *Henry IV Parts 1 & 2*, *His Dark Materials* (Royal National Theatre, dir Nicholas Hytner), and *Hamlet* (Old Vic, dir Trevor Nunn). Television credits include *Houswewife 49*, *The Great Escape* (*The Untold Story*) and *Northern Echoes*.

## Simon Sturgess
### ATC Production Manager

Simon is a freelance Production Manager and has worked with many companies including Paines Plough, Graeae, The Gogmagogs, Cheek by Jowl, Nigel Charnock Company, LIFT, Quicksilver, Opera Circus and theatre-rites. He has worked on around ten productions for ATC as Stage Manager and Production Manager, most recently *A Brief History of Helen of Troy* in 2005.

## Matt Wilde  *Director*

Matt is a former Associate Director at the National Theatre Studio and has worked extensively as a Staff and Associate director for the National Theatre and Out of Joint. Theatre includes: *On Tour* by Gregory Burke (Royal Court & Liverpool Everyman), *Slow Time* by Roy Williams (RNT Education Tour), *His Dark Materials* as revival co-director (NT Olivier) *Portugal* (rehearsed reading RNT Cottesloe),

*Criminals* (RNT Studio), *The Insatiate Countess* (Young Vic Studio), *Romeo and Juliet* and *Macbeth* (Southwark Playhouse). He is involved in developing and presenting new writing with RNT Studio, British Council, Goldsmith's College, Royal Court YWP, Liverpool Everyman & Playhouse and RADA.

ATC was founded in 1979 to tour innovative work throughout the UK. Over the years the company has developed a tradition of ensemble excellence and a reputation for originality and internationalism, picking up many awards along the way. Since Gordon Anderson and Emma Dunton joined the company in 2001 ATC has focused upon contemporary work and forged dynamic partnerships with companies and artists from across the world.

In the Autumn of 2005 ATC presented the UK premiere of *A Brief History of Helen of Troy* by Mark Schultz which was performed at Soho Theatre in London to rave reviews. Other recent productions include: *Jeff Koons* by German playwright Rainald Goetz on a UK tour and at the Institute of Contemporary Arts in London; the UK premiere of Catalan comedy *Excuses!* by Joel Joan and Jordi Sanchez in co-production with Barcelona based theatre company Krampack; *Country Music* and *One Minute* by award winning British playwright Simon Stephens in co-production with the Royal Court Theatre and Sheffield Crucible Theatre.

ATC has also produced *Arabian Night* by Roland Schimmelpfennig, *Out Of Our Heads* by comedy writer-performers Susan & Janice and Bernard Marie Koltes' *In the Solitude of Cotton Fields* in a site-specific performance at the disused Aldwych Underground station on the Strand.

*Gizmo Love* premieres at the Assembly Rooms in Edinburgh in August 2006 and then tours to Trinity Theatre Tunbridge Wells, Theatre Royal Plymouth and Birmingham Repertory Theatre.

**'Really really incredible…intricately detailed…amazing…this is a remarkable American play…'**          ★★★★★ Time Out 'Critics Choice' (*Helen of Troy*)

ATC, Malvern House
15-16 Nassau Street
London
W1W 7AB
T: 020 7580 7723  F: 020 7580 7724
E: atc@atc-online.com
www.atc-online.com

ATC is funded by the Arts Council England

# GIZMO love

First published in 2006 by Oberon Books Ltd
521 Caledonian Road, London N7 9RH
Tel: 020 7607 3637 / Fax: 020 7607 3629
e-mail: info@oberonbooks.com
www.oberonbooks.com

A catalogue record for this book is available from the British Library.

Cover image by Tim Sutton

ISBN: 1 84002 685 5

Printed in Great Britain by Antony Rowe Ltd, Chippenham.

for Hollis Melville Kolvenbach

# Characters

RALPH

MANNY

MAX

THOMAS

[Square brackets indicate a change of tone.]

# Scene 1

*RALPH, in an office that is not his own.*

RALPH: You're in a desert. A really big desert. It's so big you can't see the edge of it on any side, it goes on and on forever in all directions. (*Beat.*) And it's quiet. Nothing moves. Not even a grain of sand budges a muscle, or even *thinks* about moving is how quiet it is. Nobody Moves. (*Beat.**) Except this bug. This little bug who hasn't had any breakfast and he's starving to death, his little bug stomach is growling and his bug cupboards are totally bare and so he very carefully and slowly pokes up one antenna, up out of his hole 'cause he's *dying* of the hunger and so he takes the tiniest little step outside and WA-BANG, SNUFF. (*Beat.*) A boot. From like out of the *sky* and right down on his little bug head, squishing out his brains on the ground and squishing out his little thoughts of a delicious breakfast right out onto the sand, This Enormous Boot. BOOM. (*Beat.*) Then there's a leg. And you think it's gonna be the leg of, like, a *Mastodon*, with hair and really gross, you're expecting something *Mad* and *Evil* to be attached to this boot and you're afraid and the desert sun is blinding you so you can't really see who it *Is* or even *What* it is and Then All of a Sudden You *Can.* (*Beat.*) All of a sudden you see her. Rising up out of this big bad boot, You See Her. (*Beat.*) And it was quiet in the desert but now there's music. It was still but now the wind whips her hair and the tumble weeds rumble and the animals let loose with a barbershop wail and the earth begins to crack and heave because out of the sky THERE SHE IS. (*Beat.*) It's Doreen. Down from heaven, It's Doreen.

---

* *RALPH finds and quickly bends a paper clip. It is the bug. He places it on the ground.*

*MANNY enters holding a suitcase, talking to someone off stage. A blinding white light pours through the open doorway.*

MANNY: just a pot of coffee right away sweetie thanks soon as you get a chance. (*MANNY notices RALPH.*) Oh. Scuse me. (*MANNY exits, calling off.*) Hey.

*A pause.*

(*From off.*) Well he's *eleven*, is why.

*MANNY enters. Pause.*

Well Je-sus Christ. A boy wonder. I shoulda guessed it.

RALPH: hi.

MANNY: I thought pseudonym, first I heard about it, thought it was Falding, the bastard.

RALPH: who?

MANNY: Then I saw the fucking thing, the script, I guess, whatever you wanna call it, I thought it was a joke, a hoax, No offense, it was *me*, I couldn't see what it *was*, my own stupidity.

RALPH: Oh.

MANNY: But He had called, He *asked* me, I had no choice, I plowed through and my *God*, I gotta say, I have never in my fucking *life*, [though half the time I have no idea what you're *doing*,] I've been dying to ask you, What *is* it?

RALPH: What's what?

MANNY: Excuse me?

RALPH: ok.

MANNY: I'm Honored. Ralph, It is a Fucking Pleasure, I cannot tell you. (*Extending his hand.*) Manny McCain.

RALPH: hi.

MANNY: You should hear what He's *Saying*, My *God*, You're the Second Coming.

RALPH: I can't tell what you're talking about.

MANNY: He's blowing your *trumpet*, not since *Homer*, I heard some guy saying.

RALPH: It's my fault, probably, I can be a little off-kilter.

MANNY: and He *Loves* you. You're a made man, you don't realize, He says you're good. [You know what that *is*?] You can retire, essentially, You should be ecstatic.

RALPH: ok.

MANNY: This *Thing*, once we *fix* this thing [and we Will] we make it *recognizable*, it is a fucking *Masterpiece*. [I told you, listen, I don't pretend to *get* all of it, you'll have to excuse me, I'm moronic] but *Jesus* what I Do Get, I had trouble *Breathing*.

*Beat.*

RALPH: Can I ask you something?

MANNY: It's what I'm here for.

RALPH: Can I ask you a question?

MANNY: Absolutely.

RALPH: Who *are* you?

*Pause.*

MANNY: what's that mean.

RALPH: I'm not sure who you *are.*

> *Beat.*

MANNY: Oh you sonovabitch. A joke. Yank the old man, right? Good, ok, Eat me.

RALPH: I've been trying to figure it out this whole time I've been wondering.

MANNY: Wait. You're the guy. This is you, 'Gizmo Love' is you, right? You're Ralph?

RALPH: I'm Ralph, yes.

MANNY: He… [Wait a fucking hold on a Minute here] He hasn't *Mentioned* me?

RALPH: Not so far.

MANNY: Don't tell me this.

RALPH: ok.

MANNY: Manny McCain. 'M' little 'c' big 'C'? He hasn't *spoken* to you about me?

RALPH: Maybe he forgot?

MANNY: Oh Jesus Christ. (*Off. A roar.*) [BRING ME COFFEE!]

RALPH: Maybe he's just about to, I bet he's busy.

MANNY: God*dammitt.*

RALPH: Or there was a mix up.

MANNY: Fuckity *Fuck* Mother. You got a cigarette? [One thing, he writes. I don't even know, you tell me, is this *writing* what this is? Twenty-*three* majors I've had a hand in and I'm second Fiddle to a Third Grader.]

RALPH: sorry.

MANNY: So am I, Ralph. (*Off.*) [COFFEE, DAMMITT. *TWO* Creams.] He's always liked me, am I wrong? I have *always* done the job. God*dammitt.* I am Envied. People would *kill* for my access. I have a phone in my *house* He calls me on, in my *Den*, I may be naked when He calls, do you know this? He calls and I May Be *Naked.*

RALPH: I didn't realize that, no.

MANNY: And *This* now, I'm ugly stepsister to a…what, to a…to a…

RALPH: Third grader?

MANNY: I used that.

RALPH: Infant?

MANNY: Yes, To a Fucking INFANT. [You demand respect in this business, lemme tell you something, you ask for Coffee? You make sure it comes, you don't sit around with your thumb in your ass –]

*MANNY has moved to the door, with the intention of leaving. Just before he arrives, we hear the door being locked from the outside. MANNY tries the door, it doesn't budge.*

What's with *this* now?

RALPH: It's locked.

MANNY: Yes Ralph, it's Locked. [Jesus, and they give the kid the keys to the kingdom.] –

*The phone rings. MANNY and RALPH freeze.*

Oh *shit.*

RALPH: It's the phone.

MANNY: God*dammitt.* I am *Not* feeling well.

RALPH: Should I answer it?

MANNY: Yes answer it, it's ringing. It rings, we get it, it's a *phone* for Fucksake.

RALPH: (*Reaching for the phone.*) Ok.

MANNY: *Don't* touch that.

RALPH: It's Him.

MANNY: I know who it *is.* (*MANNY picks up the phone, hands it to RALPH.*) Here.

RALPH: (*Into the phone.*) Hello?

MANNY: ['Hello,' he says, and they got him canonized.]

RALPH: (*To MANNY.*) He wants to talk to you.

MANNY: Oh god. Oh mother of Christ. (*Then, into phone.*) Hi, sorry, listen, I'm terribly– (*Pause.*) You're kidding. (*Beat. MANNY is deeply pleased.*) *Really*? Excuse me, not to question your sincerity –

RALPH: What's he saying?

MANNY: (*Into the phone.*) No, it is *My* pleasure, is whose pleasure it is. (*Beat.*) No. Thank *You* very much. (*Beat.*) Yes. Yes me too, as am I.

*MANNY hangs up the phone.*

[Sonovabitch. Will you look at me go.] Whattayou say we get to *work.*

RALPH: Doing what?

MANNY: (*He opens his suitcase and removes a weathered wooden box. It contains writing, illustrations, sculpture, etc. 'Gizmo Love' is scrawled in crayon across the top.*) First of all, this: It's Fucking Brilliant.

RALPH: Hey, my story!

MANNY: It is one thing Ralph, it is a Fucking Masterpiece.

RALPH: (*Reaching for the Gizmo box.*) Can I have that?

MANNY: Yes, in a second, I'd like to say something.

RALPH: How did you get it?

MANNY: How did I *get* it?

RALPH: He let you see it?

MANNY: Of course He let me see it.

RALPH: Can I have it?

MANNY: In a *Second*, I've got a little something prepared.

RALPH: Right now can I have it?

MANNY: Fine, *OK*, *take* it, Jesus –

RALPH: (*Accepting the box.*) You *Read* this?

MANNY: Yes I *read* it.

RALPH: Did you like it?

MANNY: Yes I *liked* it, it's what I'm *saying* if you would shut *up*, It's Brilliant.

RALPH: (*Looking through the Gizmo box.*) Where's the dog, have you seen it? That they find? It's made of a spool. Oh boy, I hope it's not *lost*. (*Beat. RALPH pulls a single scrap of tattered paper from the box.*) Hey! Here's the part where Doreen tricks Clever out of forty dollars. Did you read that part?

MANNY: Ralph. Let's have an understanding: I read *all* of it.

19

RALPH: Why?

MANNY: *Why?*

RALPH: It gripped you by the *throat*! You couldn't put it *down*! Oh, Here. (*RALPH holds up a little sculpture.*) He's a mutt, see? But mostly shepherd I'm guessing.

MANNY: Ralph. *If.* We are going to work on this thing. *If.* You and I are going to remain friends [which I hope we do, I enjoy you–

RALPH: Work on this, whattayou mean work on this.

MANNY: I mean work on the *script.*

RALPH: How do you mean, Work on it?

MANNY: I mean *fix* it. Rewrite it. I mean we're going to *work* on it.

RALPH: You want to Change it.

*Beat.*

MANNY: Yes, Ralph.

RALPH: Change what Happens, you mean. You want to Change it.

MANNY: Yes. Sometimes we will.

RALPH: Now *wait* a *minute.*

MANNY: Listen: I understand.

RALPH: Hold *On* a *Minute.*

MANNY: Ralph? I have been there and back. I'm a writer.

RALPH: You're a changer.

MANNY: This reaction? I am in total understanding.

RALPH: I don't *know* you.

MANNY: You feel attacked.

RALPH: You could be *anybody.*

MANNY: I could be a *hack.* So What, they bring in a Hack to fuck up your masterpiece?

RALPH: I didn't agree to this.

MANNY: Who would? Did Christ? Probably not.

RALPH: (*Referring to the Gizmo box.*) It's how I like it. This is what I want it to be like al*ready.*

MANNY: Because it's brilliant. Ralph? Don't Compromise A Fucking Word.

*Beat.*

RALPH: excuse me?

MANNY: If you ruin one *morsel* of this thing, if you let Them destroy one hair on its head, I will find you, personally, and kill you.

RALPH: …that was sort of my plan.

MANNY: There are people out there who would destroy you Ralph, out of jealousy, who would fuck you. I am not those people.

RALPH: I guess that's good.

MANNY: I want to offer you something.

RALPH: No thank you.

MANNY: I want to offer you a deal.

RALPH: Nice of you to offer, but no thanks.

MANNY: We both want one thing. A great movie. Will you
Do This: Work with me to make a great movie. And
*If* [here's the part] *If* at any time, you are unhappy,
displeased, if you dis*like* what we've rewritten –

RALPH: What we've changed.

MANNY: Changed, fine, If you feel even Luke Warm, if
it doesn't light you *up*. We will *scrap* it, at Any Time,
on *your* say so, it will go back, *Exactly*, to how you first
wrote it.

*Beat.*

That's it. That's my offer. Now you respond.

RALPH: What do *I* get?

*Beat.*

MANNY: Pardon?

RALPH: I don't get what I get.

MANNY: I just said it. Veto, is what you get, you have the
final word.

RALPH: I already have that.

MANNY: Excuse me?

RALPH: I'm holding it. Right now it's that already, this is
just how I want it.

*Pause.*

MANNY: You know, I'm going to tell you something. [I
could fucking kill myself, what I am forced to *do* in this
business.] Do you know who I am? What I *Offer* you? I
am *Envied*. [This is crass, I know, but Fuck You –

*The phone rings.*

*Dammitt.*

RALPH: Uh oh.

MANNY: There it *is* again, I hope you're happy.

RALPH: Should I get it?

MANNY: Yes. And Tell him what happened.

RALPH: (*Reaching for the phone.*) Ok.

MANNY: *Don't* touch that.

*MANNY picks up the receiver.*

(*Into the phone.*) I'm sorry, I know, I'm trying, he won't – (*Beat. Then MANNY hands the phone to RALPH.*) Here.

RALPH: (*Into the phone.*) Hello? (*Pause. RALPH deflates.*)

*RALPH hangs up the phone.*

(*Quietly.*) …He says I sold it.

*Beat.*

He owns it. He says I'm a courtesy. He says I sold it and it's just a courtesy from Him, my being here even. He said it's like you sell your car, whoever buys it can drive it into a tree if He wants.

MANNY: I'm sorry Ralph.

RALPH: Or He can *never* drive it. He can leave it in his garage and never drive it. He said I should count my blessings.

MANNY: I'm sorry.

RALPH: Is that true?

MANNY: Did you take a check?

23

RALPH: I thought it would be a movie.

MANNY: Then it's true, Ralph.

> RALPH *walks to the door, tries it, finds it locked.*

Ralph?

RALPH: (*Quietly.*) I've been watching it, in my head, since I was born, practically. I can't remember ever not thinking about it.

MANNY: I know.

RALPH: They're my family.

MANNY: I understand.

RALPH: It's what I always think about. It sort of *is* my *mind*, really.

MANNY: And you sold it.

RALPH: I thought [it's so stupid] I thought if it was a *movie*, if somebody *else* could see it, I might talk to them about Doreen and Tony, a whole bunch of us would Laugh about the Mustache part, [Did you think that was funny, the mustache part?]

MANNY: Very.

RALPH: I thought if I could show it. I thought: what if other people saw it, other people, watching it and *understanding...*

MANNY: You would feel less alone.

RALPH: I would?

MANNY: That's what you thought. By showing it, by showing yourself, you would feel less alone.

*Beat.*

RALPH: I hate Him. [Is that ok to tell you?] If He was here now? I think I could murder.

MANNY: Ralph, I can't tell you how many times.

*Beat.*

RALPH: I can't feel my feet.

MANNY: Ralph.

RALPH: I'm starting to panic.

MANNY: It's not over. It can *be*, Ralph. We can *make* it.

RALPH: oh, I dunno.

MANNY: It can be *saved*. It's Possible.

*Pause.*

Ralph.

RALPH: I guess I don't really have any choices.

MANNY: Yeah well, that's how they do it.

RALPH: If I wanna...have a *part*, even, If I even wanna have a *say*, then I guess we *have* to.

*Beat.*

We have to try and *save* it. (*Beat.*) Right? Don't we, Manny? Don't we have to try and Save it?

MANNY: ask me, Ralph.

*Pause.*

You're going to have to ask me.

*Beat.*

RALPH: Will you help me Manny?

MANNY: Yes Ralph. Yes I will.

RALPH: Thank you.

MANNY: (*Pulling papers from his briefcase.*) Alright. Now. Page one.

*Lights.*

## Scene 2

*MANNY and RALPH working in the office. Later.*

MANNY: Terrific. Now read the old thing. Tony's on a rampage. He barges in, hair on fire, what does he say.

RALPH: 'Give me the fucking money.'

MANNY: Not bad. Now let's hear it with the change.

RALPH: 'Give me the money, Motherfucker.'

MANNY: *Ah.*

RALPH: Seems about the same.

MANNY: *Ralph.* Can't you see that? Don't you see what that gives us?

RALPH: I guess Not.

MANNY: The *Relationship* is what it gives us. You had: 'Give me the effing money' which is great, You've spelled out his need. He needs the money, so 'Give me the blanking money.' Fine. But *now* we *add* a layer. Now it's: 'Give me the money mother*fucker*.' Now we understand Tony's *contempt*. His *feeling* about the cashier. Calls him

names, makes reference to his family. See how I'm
going here?

RALPH: I think so.

MANNY: Now, Why *is* that? That's the new question. Why
does he treat this guy this way?

RALPH: He wants the money from the register.

MANNY: But why does he call him insulting names?

RALPH: I don't know, you just put that in there, I just found
out about that.

MANNY: Why did I *do* that, Ralph. What do we now
*understand* about Tony's feelings about the cashier?

RALPH: He doesn't like him?

MANNY: Right, good, and *why* is what we're after. Who's
the cashier.

RALPH: Roger.

MANNY: Ok Roger whattawe know about Roger.

RALPH: He's a cashier, Manny. He hates everyone. His
whole life is a countdown, 'How many seconds until I
can quit this stupid job.' (*Pulling an item from the box.*)
See? Here's his stamps.

MANNY: His what?

RALPH: Roger's stamp collection, Manny. I thought you
said you read it.

MANNY: I did read it, the guy's in the movie for about three
seconds.

RALPH: This one he got off a postcard from when Dominic went to Halifax, This he just found lying around but he liked it. See? It's a tulip.

MANNY: Why is this pertinent, Ralph?

RALPH: You don't want to look?

MANNY: Why is it *pertinent*?

RALPH: It's his *stamps*.

MANNY: Why does it *matter*?

RALPH: He *loves* them, Manny. They're the only thing in his *life*. It's a *Tulip*.

MANNY: Ralph. The guy's a cashier. He hates his job. Tony puts a gun to his head and demands the money. But Roger won't give him the money, So Tony Blows His Head Off. *Why*, Ralph. Why not just give him the money?

RALPH: It's because of the stamps.

MANNY: How is that *possible*?

RALPH: His collection is in the drawer, right under where they put the twenties, in that little slot, so Roger knows that if he gives Tony the money, then Tony'll probably take the stamps.

MANNY: Ralph.

RALPH: 'Cause they're worth money.

MANNY: Ralph?

RALPH: It's four stamps, so that's what, a dollar and thirty-four cents.

MANNY: Ralph. How do we *know* this?

RALPH: I told you.

MANNY: We the audience.

RALPH: *Oh*, we the *audience*. I guess there's no way we could know that.

MANNY: That is what I'm *Saying*. That people *care* about this stuff, There's a *hole* and some guy is gonna be *sitting* there, in the theater with his *date*, he's gonna lean over and say, 'Why not just give him the money?'

RALPH: God, people are gonna *see* this, I can't believe it. You think they'll like it?

MANNY: People *Know*, Ralph. Dammitt you can Not [Remind me of this, I forget it myself] You can*not* Underestimate Your Audience. Important question: Who'll see this movie? What's your target?

RALPH: …Scientists?

MANNY: What?

RALPH: I said scientists.

MANNY: That's an odd thing to say, Ralph, why do you say that.

RALPH: I was thinking of a group of smart people not to underestimate.

MANNY: Scientists. Terrific. Not exactly right though, given the externals, why don't we say, what: Suburban Teenage Boys.

RALPH: ok.

MANNY: Did you go to school Ralph? [Of course you did, don't answer that] Can you remember how *perceptive* you were? When you were fourteen, say?

RALPH: Fourteen. So that would be what, ninth grade. Lemme think a second.

MANNY: Say yes Ralph, please, for argument's sake.

RALPH: 'Oh sure, I remember.'

MANNY: Now let me tell you something: [Follow this Ralph, This was told to me.] You show a fourteen year old kid, let's say a fourteen year old suburban white kid, you show this kid a movie.

RALPH: ok.

MANNY: A Western. [Stick with me here Ralph, this is a Quiz]

RALPH: Oh good.

MANNY: Here's the scene: The hero walks into a bar, he's full of quiet fury. [You know the thing, decent guy, peaceable rancher, pushed to his limits, resorts to violence, you'd do the same given the circumstances.] So the hero walks in, and Holy Shit, there's the villain. The hero pulls out a Knife. A machete, say, and he Lops the villain's head off, Clean Off at the neck, alright? The Head goes flying through the air, There it is, it's sort of Floating, like a Blimp, *suspended* in air. Boom, you cut to the bartender, he screams, 'ahh,' Boom, cut back to the hero holding the machete, blood dripping, maybe a piece of the spine stuck to the blade. Then boom: hero turns, walks out, into the sunset, Scene. Now: [Quiz time, here it comes Ralph] What. What does our fourteen year old say?

RALPH: What does he say?

MANNY: He's at the movie with his date, paid good money Ralph, this kid who *you* think you can *fool*, sees this scene, what does he say.

*Beat.*

RALPH: 'What happened to the head?'?

MANNY: [Ladies and gentlemen I have a screenwriter in my possession.] What Happened to the *Head*.

RALPH: It's still floating.

MANNY: We underestimated our audience, Ralph, we left a head floating in the bar.

RALPH: Like a blimp.

MANNY: Yes, thank you, like a blimp.

RALPH: We never showed it landing.

MANNY: We should have, Boom: cut to the head floating, then Boom: Splat. It lands on the bar.

RALPH: In the olives.

*Beat.*

MANNY: What?

RALPH: Maybe it lands in the olives?

MANNY: How would that happen?

RALPH: I was just thinking, it could land in the martini olives, make a noise.

MANNY: Have you *been* to a bar, Ralph?

RALPH: um.

MANNY: You know what? I'm going to give you a project: Notice Things. It's what a writer does, Ralph. We're observers.

RALPH: It shouldn't land in the olives?

MANNY: How big is the olive thing, Ralph. The cup, the glass, the olive container. Say it's a theme bar, a science bar, for your target audience of *scientists*, say they keep olives in a *beaker*, how big is the Olive Beaker?

RALPH: Not big enough for a head to land in?

MANNY: No it's not. It's not big enough for a head to land in.

RALPH: Oh boy.

MANNY: (*Yelling off.*) [Can we get some Fucking Coffee in Here Please if it's not too much trouble?]

RALPH: Hey Manny?

MANNY: (*Yelling off.*) [We're *Thirsty*, Jesus, Is it so much to *Ask.*]

RALPH: I'm starting to wonder what I'm even *doing* here.

*Beat.*

MANNY: excuse me?

RALPH: I dunno. You keep talking about what a writer does and what one *is* and I have to tell you, None of that stuff sounds anything *like* me.

MANNY: Ralph.

RALPH: This is all I know, is this one story and if you happen to ask me about the *mole* behind Doreen's *ear*, I can tell you exactly what it looks like. But then the rest of this stuff… In my actual life, Manny, no ones ever knows what I'm *talking* about. I don't even *expect* anyone *ever* to know what I'm *saying*. My story makes sense in my *head*, but as far as the actual *world* goes, I don't think I'm the guy to *ask*.

MANNY: You're discouraged.

RALPH: I'm not sure I'm even *good* at this.

MANNY: C'mere.

RALPH: I haven't *been* to a lot of places, Manny, I'm not even sure what half this stuff *looks* like.

MANNY: Ralph sit.

*RALPH sits next to MANNY.*

RALPH: Plus they won't let us drink any coffee, or take a shower, and I'm getting kind of *tired*, I sort of just feel like going *home*.

MANNY: You wanna know what I write about?

*Pause.*

Whatever the scene is, a family having dinner, a gunfight. It could be in outer space, I always write about the same thing.

RALPH: what's that.

MANNY: Phyllis Kaplan.

*Beat.*

RALPH: Who?

MANNY: This girl from high school. She sat across from me in Chemistry. Phyllis Kaplan. (*Beat.*) Jesus Ralph, the sweaters, the perfume she wore. I spent ten years in drugstores trying to figure out what kind it was.

RALPH: Was she your girlfriend?

MANNY: She never spoke to me. Never looked at me. I tried a couple of times, more than once, but she never acknowledged me. (*Beat.*) I wanted her more than I've ever wanted anything in my life. That's what I write about, Ralph.

*Beat.*

So you've never been to Paris. Who gives a shit. The scene's not gonna work because you know what *wine* they're drinking. It doesn't work because you understand the *cheese*, Ralph. It works because the guy in the café wants her more than he's ever wanted anything in his life.

*Beat.*

RALPH: It works because of Phyllis.

*Beat.*

MANNY: You are ungot, Ralph. Adrift in the world. No one has any idea what you're talking about. And you have a story you wanna tell that burns a hole in your heart. You know what I think? I think I have an author on my hands.

*Lights.*

# Scene 3

*A Hideout.*

*MAX and THOMAS enter, wearing twin white jumpsuits. THOMAS' jumpsuit is stained with fresh blood.*

MAX: How many times are we going to go *through* this?

THOMAS: [At least one more, it looks like.]

MAX: You have a Passive Subject, Thomas, He had *soiled* himself for Godssake.

THOMAS: I know, that was disgusting.

MAX: Did you *look* at this guy? Before you decide to *shoot* him for no reason?

THOMAS: I didn't *decide* anything –

MAX: He was a *Nanny.*

THOMAS: I didn't *decide* Max, It was instinct.

MAX: It was *what?*

THOMAS: I had an instinct.

MAX: (*Beat.*) [You know, you'd think, over a *lifetime*, you like to believe that at least *some* of what you offer might actually be *received* –

THOMAS: Can we change the subject here, Max?

MAX: He was *Compliant.*

THOMAS: I don't think so.

MAX: He shit his *pants*, Thomas, this *Enthusiast*, What do you *want?*

THOMAS: He Moved.

*Beat.*

MAX: Do you forget that I was *Standing* there? that I was Standing Right There?

THOMAS: I saw him move.

MAX: He Did *Not* [and even if he *had*, so a man, picked last his whole *life*, this guy scratches his *elbow* –

THOMAS: I'm not saying he scratched his elbow.

MAX: He was *Compliant*! On my *request*, this man Unlocked his own *Door*. I had only to *Ask*!

THOMAS: 'Get outta the cah.'

*Beat.*

MAX: Excuse me?

THOMAS: That's how you said it. 'Get outta de cah.'

MAX: What in Sam Hill are you talking about.

THOMAS: I was Standing there.

MAX: That is *not* how I say that.

THOMAS: 'Get outta de cah.'

MAX: Are you *joking*? An Accent? Why would I do that?

THOMAS: I don't know.

MAX: In a *Professional Situation*, I'm a Vaudevillian? What are you saying? I'm an *Impressionist*?

THOMAS: Sometimes when we're on a job –

MAX: What *is* this? '*Sometimes*'? You've got a fucking Theory here Thomas? You've got *Examples*?

THOMAS: I've *noticed* something.

MAX: You're a spy. You watch me *Sleep*, You take my *Pulse* when I'm *Napping*, you have a *Chart*.

THOMAS: Now don't get all crazy.

MAX: Who you *Shot* this guy, by the way, while we're slinging arrows, I may have *mispronounced*, which I *didn't*, I made a *request*, in *Accepted Parlance* – [You think I'm a *Cartoon*? What do I *gain*? In front of a *subject*, Thomas?] Why Would I Do that?

THOMAS: you want them to love you.

> *Pause.*

It's what I think, Max.

> *Pause.*

MAX: Thomas, Christ.

THOMAS: It might be one of those unconscious things.

MAX: good Lord.

THOMAS: You might not be *aware* of it.

MAX: Thomas.

THOMAS: It's only *natural*, a guy wants to be appreciated.

MAX: I have *you*.

> *Pause.*

THOMAS: [You *have* me, you said?]

MAX: I need love? It's what you're saying: Max tries to please, Max needs love from strangers.

THOMAS: Ok.

MAX: and I'm saying well how about this: I have you.

*Pause.*

THOMAS: Oh.

MAX: Right?

THOMAS: Max. Thank you very much.

MAX: You're welcome.

*Pause.*

THOMAS: I have you too.

MAX: Yes you do.

*Lights.*

# Scene 4

*RALPH and MANNY in the office. Much later. RALPH sits, aping Tony in the car. MANNY paces.*

MANNY: So, we're in the car, Tony's in intense pain.

RALPH: (*As Tony.*) 'Ow. My *Leg.*'

MANNY: He's cursing the cop.

RALPH: He hates cops.

MANNY: Right, and now especially 'cause his leg is a blood geyser.

RALPH: Plus, Manny, the bullet's still in his leg, it's like a part of the cop *lodged* inside his thigh proper.

MANNY: So he's doing, what, about a hundred.

RALPH: A hundred and *ten* more like, 'cause Doreen's waiting at the underpass.

MANNY: Imagine the blood geyser Ralph, it's all over the windshield.

RALPH: So he's pissed.

MANNY: He's Furious.

RALPH: Yeah, you're right Manny, He's *Furious.*

MANNY: So what would he be *saying* here?

RALPH: Something good.

MANNY: I'm assuming that.

RALPH: Something just right.

MANNY: Something with 'Fuck,' I get the feeling. Do you sense that?

RALPH: ok.

MANNY: So 'fuck' something. [fuckthis, fuckthisshit, fuckit*all*, what, *every*thing, *you*, *fuck*you, everybody, *Me*, *Fuck* Me]: Hey. How about 'fuck *me*'? Does 'fuck me' work for you?

RALPH: mm, I dunno.

MANNY: You're right, that is *awful, Dammitt.*

RALPH: [I'm getting really *hungry.*]

MANNY: something with 'fuck.' You know an *adjective* has sometimes worked, or as a kind of *gerund,* can be *very* effective.

RALPH: (*RALPH has pulled a plain yellow piece of construction paper from the Gizmo box. He holds it up.*) This is the scenery outside the car. See, Manny? They're in Kansas. It's wheat.

MANNY: Or maybe just 'Fucking fuck.' [Focus, Ralph.] 'Fucking fuck.' You think that's self-conscious, if we have him say that? We don't want to get into an ego thing, I've been accused of that, trying to draw attention to the *words*, to my*self*, to the Poetry of it.

RALPH: Can you hold this wheat up for me Manny?

MANNY: Or 'fuck' and a deity is usually pretty good: 'Jesus blanking H Christ' I've heard, 'God blanking dammitt.'

RALPH: *Hey*, I sort of *like* that.

MANNY: That might *Work*!

RALPH: 'God blanking *damm*itt.' Here, lemme try it if you hold the wheat up.

MANNY: 'God blanking *damm*itt'!

*The phone rings.*

Oh for *Godssake.*

RALPH: Leave us *Alone*!

MANNY: God*dammitt.*

RALPH: If he would not *pester* us for a minute.

MANNY: We could get something *Done.*

RALPH: We're *Working.*

MANNY: He thinks this *helps*?

RALPH: Calling all the time?

MANNY: He thinks it *soothes* us?

RALPH: Does he know *Anything*?

MANNY: About the creative process?

RALPH: About what it *takes*?

MANNY: He has not a Single *Notion*.

RALPH: Moron!

MANNY: Of what is *Required*.

RALPH: (*With sudden purpose.*) I've had *Enough*.

MANNY: He thinks he's Louis the Fourteenth? [Powdered *Wigs!*] He's a *Patron*? These people had I*Q*s! They did Not *Call* every Five Fucking *Sec*onds – Woa Ralph, what are you doing?

RALPH: (*Holds a chair above his head, ready to smash the phone to smithereens.*) Stand back, Manny, and cover your face.

MANNY: What are you *Doing*?

RALPH: Get behind me.

MANNY: Ralph, hold on a second.

RALPH: (*Winding up.*) Leave, Us, ALONE –

MANNY: *RALPH.*

*Pause. RALPH holds the chair, poised above the phone.*

(*Quietly.*) [Ralph put the chair down, Jesus Christ.]

RALPH: [What am I *doing*?]

MANNY: [What are you doing?]

RALPH: (*Lowering the chair.*) [Oh my *God*.]

MANNY: [Were you really going to *do* that?]

RALPH: [I don't know, I think I may *have*.]

MANNY: [Jesus, you gotta watch yourself.]

RALPH: [Sorry. I'm sort of losing it a little.]

MANNY: [You know you can't *do* that.]

RALPH: [no, I know, I don't know what came over me.]

MANNY: [You can't just completely lose your *Marbles, Jesus.*]

RALPH: (*Answers the phone.*) Hello? (*Beat.*) Yeah, sorry about that, we stepped out for a second.

MANNY: (*Sotto.*) Woa Ralph, We stepped *out*?

RALPH: (*Into the phone.*) Or I guess we nodded off.

MANNY: (*Sotto.*) *Ralph.*

RALPH: (*Into the phone.*) It was a quick nap and then the ringing woke us.

MANNY: (*Sotto.*) Here gimme that, lemme talk to him.

RALPH: (*Into the phone.*) No, it's going *great*! (*Beat.*) No, He *is*, a *Lot.* (*Beat.*) No he's Doing Great, he really is, I *swear.* (*Beat.*) ok. (*RALPH hangs up the phone.*)

*Pause.*

MANNY: What did he say?

RALPH: nothing. He was mad that it rang so many times.

MANNY: What did he say.

RALPH: He's fine, He wanted to know how we're doing.

MANNY: Ralph? What did he Say.

RALPH: Nothing. 'Keep it up.'

MANNY: If you lie to me Once More. If a *Half*-truth comes from your mouth I will Tear your Throat from your Neck.

RALPH: It's O*K*, Manny.

MANNY: He SAID WHAT.

RALPH: 'Is McCain helping or is he a hindrance.'

*Beat.*

MANNY: Oh for Crying Out Loud can I get Some *Mercy*?

RALPH: It's O*K*.

MANNY: It is Far from *that*. It is not *nearly* OK.

RALPH: We'll ignore him.

MANNY: My life is *over*.

RALPH: I told Him we're doing fine.

MANNY: Oh, *you* told him, terrific. (*Then, yelling off.*) [I WANT A CUP OF COFFEE IN A MUG WITH A HANDLE] I'm thought *Incompetent*. He hates my *guts*, Call the kid, ask him if McCain has fucked it up yet. This is a *Disaster*.

RALPH: Manny, I think you're overreacting.

MANNY: I'm *WHAT*?

RALPH: He just wanted to know how it's going.

MANNY: Don't *Ever*. [Lemme tell you something.] My *Perceptions*, and my *Reactions* given those perceptions, this is *Who* I *Am*. You know what a writer *is*? A Writer Sees the *Truth*.

RALPH: (*Soothingly.*) Manny you're acting crazy.

MANNY: In Murky Waters, that's what a writer *Does*. I SEE TRUTH, I WRITE IT DOWN. I am OVERREACTING?

RALPH: (*Soothingly.*) You're acting like a crazy person Manny. Come on, look at yourself a second.

*Pause. MANNY sits, puts his head in his hands.*

MANNY: …oh Jesus Christ.

RALPH: (*Gently.*) You're letting things get to you a little.

MANNY: I'm falling apart.

RALPH: We haven't eaten in a while.

MANNY: You think that's it?

RALPH: Maybe you're starving to death.

MANNY: Oh mother of Christ, Ralph. I'm a little shaky.

RALPH: You're in withdrawal maybe. You wanna work on the next thing?

MANNY: No.

RALPH: It's when they find the puppy.

MANNY: You do it.

RALPH: I need you Manny, c'mon.

MANNY: I don't think I would be much help to you.

RALPH: Yes you would, c'mon, you're a genius.

MANNY: I'm a genius?

RALPH: Sure.

MANNY: Lemme let you in on a little something Ralph. (*Beat.*) You live a life.

RALPH: It's ok.

MANNY: and there it is. You wanna know who you are? What you've become? It's right there for you.

RALPH: You're a nice man.

MANNY: Your identity? It's right there, Ralph. The Facts of your life. You examine your history, what you've *done* and you're what.

RALPH: A *writer.*

MANNY: A failure? Have you failed, consistently? No, not consistently, Ralph, *every time.* In every thing you have ever tried, you have Failed. So there it is. Just look. Who am I? It's easy. Your history, your record, your Life is who you Are.

*Pause.*

RALPH: (*Pulling a piece of paper from his pocket, unfolding it.*) Manny look at this a second.

MANNY: Ralph please. No more artefacts, Ok?

RALPH: Look at this one.

MANNY: Half the time I can't tell what the hell you're even talking about, I pretend I do, to seem relevant. I fake it most of the time.

RALPH: Manny, just look for a second. Here.

*RALPH holds the paper in front of MANNY. MANNY looks at it, then takes it slowly into his hands. Pause.*

MANNY: …oh my God.

RALPH: No one's seen this one.

MANNY: Where did you get this?

RALPH: It's Doreen.

MANNY: I see that.

RALPH: I keep it in my pocket.

MANNY: Did you *make* this?

RALPH: It's Doreen.

MANNY: You painted this Ralph? How did you do this?

RALPH: Isn't she beautiful?

MANNY: She's…God, she's like I pictured.

RALPH: You can say hi if you want.

MANNY: Oh Ralph, she's just beautiful.

RALPH: Say hi Manny, c'mon. Introduce yourself.

*Pause.*

MANNY: Hi.

RALPH: 'Hello.'

MANNY: I'm honored.

RALPH: 'Ah, no big thing.'

MANNY: Hello Doreen.

RALPH: Doreen, this is Manny. Meet your maker.

*Lights.*

# Scene 5

*MAX and THOMAS at home.*

THOMAS: I understand what your *opinion* is, I just think something else than you.

MAX: You think I go down on that part.

THOMAS: That is what I think.

MAX: Let's go again.

THOMAS: This time try going down on that part.

MAX: I will try that this time.

*MAX and THOMAS sing the end of 'Amazing Grace' with MAX taking the low notes.*

THOMAS: (*Singing.*) I once

MAX / THOMAS: Was lost,
but now am found,
Was blind –

*A phone rings.* * *THOMAS withdraws a pistol and shoots the phone, in one swift and sure motion. The phone jumps, as if goosed. The ringing stops.*

*Beat.*

MAX: Can I ask you a question? Do I Exist?

THOMAS: We were working on the song.

MAX: What if nothing you ever do or say has any effect?

THOMAS: I'm pretty sure you exist, Max.

MAX: You move a *Chair* across the room, but you turn around and the chair hasn't budged. You split a cord of *wood*, You turn, and it's a *tree*, with *Leaves*, You devote a *Career*, many *thousands* of hours, to *Teaching*, You Invest your *life* in Passing something *On*, but I turn to you Thomas and What do I see?

THOMAS: I thought the song was finally starting to sound good.

---

* *An identical ring to the phone in the writer's office.*

MAX: So you shoot an *Appliance*? Have you heard a *word*, in All These Years, Have you understood a *syllable* of what I've Told You?

THOMAS: I don't remember this ever coming up.

MAX: What is the rule by which we live?

THOMAS: I can't think of a rule about shooting the phone.

MAX: We do what is *Necessary*.

THOMAS: yeah ok, that I remember.

MAX: I know men who are *Flamboyant*, Do you know what else they are? They are Unemployed. You wanna wear a *Scarf*? You want your picture in the *Paper*? Mark my words: You will be Unwanted.

THOMAS: I know.

MAX: We do the Job, that is what we do.

THOMAS: I'm not saying we shouldn't do the job.

MAX: You're saying we should shoot the phone.

*The phone rings.*

*Godammitt.*

THOMAS: oh boy.

MAX: *What* am I about to say.

THOMAS: I thought I got it pretty good.

MAX: Thomas. *What* Am I Going to Say To You.

THOMAS: If it becomes necessary to use lethal force, make sure the thing is all the way dead.

MAX: But that's not what you *did*.

THOMAS: I got it square, Max.

MAX: Did you?

THOMAS: That must be a really resilient phone.

MAX: You make *sure.* This is the point. You don't *Hope*, You don't *Expect*, or make an *Assumption* about the weakness of an electrical device. What should you have done.

THOMAS: Shoot it more?

MAX: Jesus, Thomas, No You don't shoot it more. It's a Phone, You want it to stop ringing, For God's Sake How about if You Take it off the *Hook*.

THOMAS: I should've taken it off the hook.

MAX: It might have *occurred* to you.

THOMAS: I see.

MAX: Before you blow up the *building*, You might unplug it.

THOMAS: I'm sorry, Max.

MAX: You test a man's patience, Thomas.

THOMAS: You want me to unplug it?

MAX: I want you to know what to do. To take many years of learning, of my *efforts*, I want you to Do what is right. That is what I want.

*Beat. THOMAS thinks.*

THOMAS: (*He picks up the phone.*) Hello?

MAX: Thank you. Excellent. Thomas? There is hope yet.

THOMAS: (*To MAX.*) Was that good?

MAX: Yes. We do the job. We take an assignment. When a phone rings, we don't fire upon it, no, we answer it. We see what He wants.

THOMAS: (*Into the phone.*) Your Bigness. What'll it be?

*Lights.*

# Scene 6

*MANNY and RALPH in the office, pacing.*

MANNY: He *hates* it.

RALPH: Manny, we only just put it through.

MANNY: With every passing second, I can hear our graves being dug.

RALPH: Maybe he's combing it over. It would take a while, maybe he likes it so *far*.

MANNY: It takes a very short time to love something, Ralph. *Hating* is what takes longer. I would know, I married an actress.

*MANNY attempts to peek through the brass mail slot which is mounted in the door. A blinding white light rushes through the slot, temporarily blinding him, nearly knocking him over.*

Jesus *Christ.*

RALPH: Oh my God.

MANNY: That is fucking bright.

RALPH: Are you OK?

MANNY: (*Staggered.*) No. I'm blind, Jesus, I can't see.

RALPH: I hope your cornea's not singed.

MANNY: Can that *happen*?

RALPH: I don't smell any burning.

MANNY: That's a relief, Ralph, thank you.

RALPH: (*Sucking on the collar of his T-shirt.*) What if he doesn't like it?

MANNY: (*Indicating RALPH's shirt sucking.*) Don't do that.

RALPH: Sorry.

MANNY: You'll stretch it out.

RALPH: I didn't know I was doing it.

MANNY: Ruin a shirt that way, stretch the collar.
[God*dammitt* what's *keeping* him, he's a *thing*, isn't he, what is he, a *Cicada*.]

RALPH: A *what*?

MANNY: You sure it's flip-flops in that last thing?

RALPH: Manny that was *your* idea, I love that idea.

MANNY: I know, I just wonder, flip-flops. Can you run in those things?

RALPH: I don't have any.

MANNY: One, Ralph. Can *one*.

RALPH: Oh. I *think* so. I think one can.

MANNY: Sometimes doesn't that thing pull through the bottom? If she's sprinting? The thing between your toes comes through, they fall apart.

RALPH: Maybe we could reinforce the stem thing, you know how people do? With a washer?

MANNY: Make it bigger.

RALPH: With a washer, so it doesn't pull through as easy.

MANNY: But would she *do* that.

RALPH: Right, would *Doreen*, probably not, she would never probably think of doing that.

MANNY: How about sandals.

RALPH: Sandals? You mean like the apostles?

MANNY: Can you picture it?

RALPH: Her foot is sort of, I dunno, *Sandals.*

MANNY: Do you have any foot renderings? Of her toes, maybe, a foot sculpture in there?

RALPH: (*RALPH moves to the Gizmo box. He forages.*) Not really. Shoulda made something, didn't think to. (*RALPH removes a wedding band from the box. He holds it up.*) This ring, only.

MANNY: Her *ankle*? Anything? What's with the ring?

RALPH: oh nothing. Her toes are *webbed*, Manny, remember? but just the third one and –

MANNY: Third and fourth, I know. What's that ring about?

RALPH: What.

MANNY: The ring Ralph, what is that?

RALPH: This? Nothing. Wanna look at some other stuff? Here's a canister of breath Tony gave her. You can only open it once.

MANNY: The ring, Ralph. Is Tony gonna propose?

RALPH: No. He wanted to but I won't let him.

MANNY: So what's with the ring? Is Doreen proposing to *him*?

RALPH: I just found it. It was just in here.

MANNY: I hope you don't expect me to believe that.

RALPH: Can we talk about something else Manny? How about let's talk about how much you're respected in this town.

MANNY: Someone's getting married?

RALPH: I'm not sure.

MANNY: Someone from the movie's getting married?

RALPH: Sort of.

MANNY: Who? Tony *dies* in the end Ralph, she can't marry a dead guy.

RALPH: It's not him who gets married to anybody.

MANNY: It's Doreen.

RALPH: Yes.

MANNY: Ralph. Who Marries Doreen?

RALPH: maybe me. (*Beat, then: Off.*) [COULD WE GET SOME COFFEE IN HERE RIGHT AWAY WE DEMAND SOME COFFEE RIGHT AWAY THIS INSTANT, COFFEE!]

   *Pause.*

MANNY: You Ralph. You and Doreen.

RALPH: yes.

MANNY: You're going to propose to Doreen?

RALPH: After Tony dies.

MANNY: *Ralph.*

RALPH: (*Openly.*) What do you think she'll say, Manny?

MANNY: Ralph, Jesus.

RALPH: I'm very nervous, I have to say, she might say no.

MANNY: *Doreen.* You do know what the deal is there.

RALPH: I'm so Strange, Manny, I'm really sort of an odd *guy.*

MANNY: Ok.

RALPH: Most people can't *see* me very well.

MANNY: Well you're *unusual.* You're off the beaten track. Still –

RALPH: Do you think she'll be able to see me?

*Beat.*

My first feeling is that she may actually be able to see me. Is that your feeling?

MANNY: Ralph, we gotta make sure of something here –

RALPH: I love her.

MANNY: Well I see that, she's very special, but as far as the actual marriage goes, in actual *reality* goes –

RALPH: Manny does your heart sing?

MANNY: My what?

RALPH: Mine hums. It kind of hums along to what's happening. Like in a movie, my heart hums a soundtrack for me. Does your heart do that?

*Pause.*

It hums along to what I'm thinking about. But then sometimes? Sometimes a hum doesn't cover it. Sometimes it has to Sing. So it opens, my heart Opens, Manny, and Belts it Out, because she's so *much*. My heart says, 'mere humming doesn't *begin*,' and it has to *Sing* Manny, my *Heart* and to *Leap*. (*Beat.*) Does your heart ever do that?

*Beat.*

MANNY: Ah, Ralph. No. Not in a while.

RALPH: Some people go to church, Manny. They believe in things. When they're alone, at night, they have someone to talk to.

MANNY: You have Doreen.

RALPH: When I'm all alone, when it's dark. She's good company.

*Pause. They think this over.*

Can I ask you something?

MANNY: Sure.

RALPH: When we get married? If we do?

MANNY: Yes?

RALPH: Will you be at the wedding?

*Beat.*

MANNY: Ralph? I would be Honored.

RALPH: Will you be my father?

*Beat.*

*The revised script flies suddenly through the mail slot. It lands heavily in the center of the floor. A yellow note is attached to its cover. Pause. MANNY and RALPH stare at the script, unmoving.*

(*Whispering.*) There's a note.

MANNY: There's a note on it Ralph.

RALPH: Can you read it?

MANNY: I can't, no, not from here.

RALPH: Me neither.

MANNY: (*Inching toward it.*) Come on.

RALPH: You go ahead.

MANNY: Come with me.

*MANNY and RALPH approach the script with great caution.*

I'm going to pick it up.

RALPH: I can't look.

MANNY: I'm going to look at the note.

RALPH: Whatever you think is best.

*Pause. MANNY reads the note. He lowers the script slowly to his side.*

What does it say?

*Pause.*

What does it say, Manny?

MANNY: It says 'no.'

RALPH: 'No.'?

MANNY: It says 'no.'

*The door swings easily open, the light pours through. MAX and THOMAS enter. MAX holds a coffee in a paper cup.*

MAX: Somebody here order coffee?

*Lights.*

*End of Act One.*

## Scene 7

*Later, in the office. MANNY and RALPH working. MAX reads the paper, THOMAS observes.* * *MANNY holds the coffee cup, half empty.*

RALPH: You think the cop part is stupid?

MANNY: I think it lacks *Veritas*, Ralph, I think it has the quality of something *Manufactured*.

RALPH: You think it's a little stupid.

MANNY: Yes I do. (*Handing the coffee to RALPH.*) [Here, drink that.] And I think it's an *Infection*, Ralph, of *Horseshit*, that has given all the other stuff a *Disease*.

RALPH: (*Referring to the coffee.*) Do you want any more? It's mostly spit.

MANNY: (*Taking the coffee.*) Sure. No, this is fine. That's good coffee.

RALPH: So once we take out the infection.

MANNY: We're surgeons, Ralph, we Extract the sonovabitch.

RALPH: Then the rest is probably ok.

MANNY: The rest is probably *great*. Is *certainly* great.

THOMAS: (*To MAX.*) [Can I have a butterscotch?]

MAX: (*Reaching into his pocket.*) [I think that last one was the last one. Nope, here you go.]

THOMAS: (*To MAX, unwrapping noisily.*) [Bit of a scratchy throat.]

---

* *MAX and THOMAS are the audience, MANNY and RALPH the show.*

MANNY: (*To RALPH, referring to MAX and THOMAS.*) This guy unwraps one more sucker, I don't know *what* I'm gonna do.

RALPH: Try and ignore them.

MANNY: If I had a *nickel* for every ounce of humiliation.

RALPH: The Infection, Manny.

MANNY: A Penny for every Pound, I'd be a rich and bitter man.

RALPH: The *Disease*, Manny, come on, we're Surgeons.

MANNY: Surgeons. Right. So what do we have.

RALPH: It's the part where the cops arrest Doreen.

MANNY: Which sucks.

RALPH: What do we need?

MANNY: Something that doesn't suck.

RALPH: Like what?

*Beat. Then MANNY crosses to the Gizmo Box, with purpose.*

MANNY: We hold the Wheat up.

RALPH: Will that help, you think?

MANNY: (*Pulling out the yellow piece of construction paper.*) It's not gonna kill us Ralph, that I *do* know.

RALPH: (*Gamely.*) Then Hold It Up, Manny.

MANNY: We *try* it.

RALPH: We're in the business of *trying* things.

MANNY: (*Moving to RALPH, holding the paper aloft between them.*) Alright. Here's the Wheat. Here's us.

RALPH: Us and Wheat. Extracting infections.

*MANNY and RALPH, with intense concentration, silently search for the solution.*

THOMAS: [It's a big world, Max.]

MAX: [Isn't that the truth.]

THOMAS: [Like for instance: What the fuck is *wrong* with these guys?]

MANNY: (*His concentration broken.*) Alright that's enough.

MAX: [Takes all kinds, I guess.]

THOMAS: [Yeah, but to a *point.*]

MANNY: (*Crossing to THOMAS and MAX.*) Ex*cuse* me. We are *working* here.

THOMAS: (*To MAX.*) Hey look, he's talking to us.

MANNY: *We –* [If I may be so bold as to interrupt the *Groundlings* for a second, if I may for a second be so *Crass*] We have a *Job* to do. [OK?] and I would *Appeal,* [given the nature of *your* assignment [being in this case identical to ours] which is to see this work *Completed*] I am going to *Ask,* Could you find it in your *Heart,* to not say *Anything, Anymore.* No *Talking.* [Can we do this?] *No Speaking.*

*Beat.*

THOMAS: (*To MAX.*) [We shoulda brought checkers.]

MAX: [Yeah, well.]

THOMAS: [Gotta remember to bring checkers next time.]

MAX: [Write it down.]

THOMAS: [Ok.]

MANNY: Jesus *Christ*!

RALPH: I think they might try to be quiet now, Manny.

MANNY: Do I have to *Demand* every *Earned* Thing?

RALPH: Yeah, it sorta seems like you do.

MANNY: Can I have an *Expectation*?

RALPH: Not so far.

MANNY: Must I *Beg* for every *Normalcy*?

THOMAS: (*As he writes, with a pen from his pocket.*) 'bring checkers.'

MANNY: How about a GRANULE of respect? Mightn't I be *Bequeathed* that?

*The phone rings.*

Oh for the love of God!

THOMAS: (*Jumping to his feet, gleefully.*) PHONE!

RALPH: I'm hiding.

THOMAS: PHONE'S RINGING!

MANNY: Is it something I Did? Could I *deserve* it somehow?

RALPH: Will no one please tell him I'm hiding?

MANNY: I'm Cursed. There is a Mark on My Soul.

THOMAS: THE TELEPHONE IS RINGING!

MANNY: I was Born to be Tortured! I am the Stickpin of the Universe!

THOMAS: PHONE!

*MAX casually picks up the phone, an act that freezes the others and ends the eruption.*

MAX: This response, I've gotta say, I've begun to question my *own* reaction. Can someone explain this to me?

*Pause. MAX holds the receiver casually by his side, awaiting an explanation. MANNY and RALPH eye him intently.*

RALPH: (*Sotto.*) Manny.

MAX: Do you people hear something I don't?

RALPH: (*Sotto.*) He's not *talking* into it.

MANNY: (*Sotto.*) I *see* that.

RALPH: (*Sotto.*) What's he *doing*?

MANNY: (*Sotto.*) I can't *tell.*

RALPH: (*Sotto.*) Does he *know* he's not talking into it?

MAX: (*Casually curious.*) Is it the *pitch* for you guys that causes this?

MANNY: (*Carefully, to MAX.*) You do realize you're holding the phone there.

MAX: (*The phone on his hip.*) Like a dog whistle? Is it that kind of thing?

MANNY: (*To MAX.*) Are you out of your *mind,* suddenly?

RALPH: Take his pulse, Manny.

MANNY: He's out of his *Tree.*

MAX: Or is it the time *between* rings? the silences.

*Pause. MANNY and RALPH gape.*

(*To himself.*) [ah, well. You can't account for strange,
I guess.] (*Then into the phone.*) yeah, Bigness, how's it
hangin'?

RALPH: (*Sotto.*) *Manny.*

MANNY: (*Staring at MAX.*) 'How is it Hanging?'!

RALPH: Did he just ask him how it's hanging?

MANNY: (*Referring to MAX, admiringly.*) Jesus *Christ*, this guy!

RALPH: I think he's demented.

MANNY: Look at him Ralph, he's a Sociopath!

MAX: (*Into the phone.*) Big? We've got a snafu of some kind,
I'm gonna have to call you back.

MANNY: Holy *Mother*!

RALPH: I don't like this.

MANNY: (*To RALPH.*) Holy *Jesus*, 'Call you *Back*!' *Ralph.* Did
you *hear* that?

RALPH: Yes.

MANNY: If I *Feel* like it, if it's *Convenient*, I will give you a
*Ring*!

RALPH: Manny.

MANNY: If I'm in the *Mood*, if it Strikes my *Fancy*!

RALPH: Manny wait a minute.

MANNY: I may not *Want* to, I might be *Occupied*, I might
be Getting My *Hair* Done, You *Earthworm*, You piece
of *Dung*, I might not fucking *Feel* Like It. Goddammitt
Ralph I am Trans*ported*! We can FIGHT THE POWER!

RALPH: I don't think that's a good idea.

MANNY: FIGHT THE POWER!

*Beat.*

THOMAS: (*To MAX.*) [Maybe they got poisoned by the coffee, it caused some kind of derangement.]

MAX: [Check the cup, see if there's a smell.]

MANNY: *Ralph.* You see what we've *got* here.

RALPH: (*Anticipating MANNY's idea.*) Oh no Manny, I dunno about that.

MANNY: We bring 'em *in*, we extract the infection.

RALPH: I don't think that's very smart.

THOMAS: (*Sniffing the coffee cup.*) [Nothing I can detect Max.]

MAX: (*Returning to his chair.*) [Alright. I guess we let 'em run.]

MANNY: He's in the flesh, Ralph. You saw it. They should lock this guy up.

RALPH: I *know.* That's exactly my *feeling.*

MANNY: So we can *tap* that.

RALPH: What if something happens?

MANNY: We praise *God.*

RALPH: Oh Manny, I don't think so.

MANNY: Ralph, please. (*Pulling him aside.*) We got Iron Ore here. We Smelt these guys [They're Raw *Material*] We *Solve* the *Scene.*

RALPH: (*Privately.*) But we don't *know* them, Manny. Already, neither one of them is one of *us*, and plus, they don't know anything *about* it.

MANNY: Ralph.

RALPH: They don't know what she *looks* like, even. (*Whispering.*) They haven't seen her *picture.*

MANNY: (*In confidence.*) But I *have*, Ralph, please. We have a *chance* with this, What we've *begged* for. Trust me. We *try* it. Come on. (*MANNY kisses RALPH gently on the forehead.*) Ralph please.

*Beat.*

RALPH: …I guess we could try it.

MANNY: Thank you. Thank you. Gentlemen? A Proposition.

RALPH: He wants you guys to be the cops in the scene with us.

MAX: (*Standing.*) Glad to.

MANNY: Really?

MAX: Sure thing. Come on Thomas.

THOMAS: (*Getting up.*) Ok.

MANNY: Fantastic.

MAX: We're the cops?

MANNY: Ralph is Doreen, you two are Cops. You have flashlights.

THOMAS: *Flash*lights, I like this already.

RALPH: We might as well just *give* 'em the stupid flashlights.

MANNY: (*Moving to the Gizmo Box, removing two homemade, working flashlights, handing them to THOMAS and MAX.*) Excellent. I have a very good feeling.

THOMAS: (*Trying his out.*) Hey this isn't stupid. Look, Max. It lights.

MAX: Will you look at that.

THOMAS: (*Privately.*) [I don't think this is stupid, Ralph.]

RALPH: [...thanks.]

THOMAS: (*To RALPH.*) [You *Made* this?]

MANNY: Thomas? I'm going to need full focus from you here.

THOMAS: Sorry.

MANNY: You two are cops.

MAX: We're cops.

MANNY: State troopers. From Kansas.

RALPH: It *might* be Kansas. It's not *necessarily* Kansas.

MANNY: Yes, sorry, you are from a place that *may* be Kansas.

RALPH: It has the *feel* of Kansas.

THOMAS: Can I ask a question?

MAX: (*Pointing to THOMAS.*) Got a question here.

THOMAS: I've never been to Kansas.

RALPH: (*To MANNY.*) Oh, see? They've never *been* there even.

MANNY: Neither have you, Ralph.

RALPH: So?

MANNY: So it's *pretend.*

THOMAS: I already knew it was pretend.

MAX: You're way ahead of 'em, T.

THOMAS: We're pretending.

RALPH: No you're *Not.* [See, Manny?] That ruins *Everything.*

MANNY: Ralph please.

MAX: (*To MANNY.*) Are we sure this is a good idea?

THOMAS: Seems like Ralph's not very happy.

MANNY: No, he is, I apologize. He's making a point. Ralph?

RALPH: What.

MANNY: Say what it is, what the point is.

RALPH: No Faking.

MANNY: Thank you. Got that fellas? No faking.

THOMAS: [I should write that down, 'no faking.']

MANNY: (*Indicating the chair and the dog sculpture.*) Now: Here's Doreen's car, and this is the dog. You guys are here. Sitting in your squad car.

MAX: We set up a speed trap.

MANNY: Dynamite. [Ok Ralph? They're looking for speeders.]

THOMAS: Or maybe not even looking, particularly. Maybe sharing a doughnut?

MANNY: *There* you go! Anticipate nothing.

THOMAS: (*Practicing.*) [Want the rest of this doughnut Max?]

MAX: [Nah, no thanks.]

THOMAS: [You sure?]

MANNY: That's good, you two.

MAX: (*To THOMAS.*) [What kind is it?]

RALPH: He looking right *at* it, Manny, he would know what *Kind* it is.

MAX: (*To MANNY.*) I'm thinking it's dark.

THOMAS: It's too dark to *see* it, Ralph.

MANNY: Yes, [Jesus] Thank you, Ok Ralph? It's Dark inside the car, he can't See what Kind it is.

THOMAS: It's cream filled.

MANNY: Tremendous. Alright. Now here we go. Ralph is Doreen, you two are cops, the puppy's the puppy. And we begin. A Dark Kansas-like night. Doreen and the Puppy *Flying* down a deserted highway. Max and Thomas, eating doughnuts, none the wiser.

THOMAS: (*To MAX, miming a doughnut.*) Want the rest of this?

MAX: I dunno, what kind is it?

MANNY: Doreen *Roars* by. A Hundred and Fifty Miles an Hour. There She Goes!

THOMAS: Holy Mother!

MAX: (*Miming a seat belt.*) Belt up, Thomas.

MANNY: The cops Pull Out. Hot Pursuit.

THOMAS: [I'll put the rest of this doughnut down, probably.]

MAX: (*Miming driving.*) *Hang* on.

THOMAS: [I won't mention putting it down, I'll just put it down.]

MANNY: SIRENS! HOLY SHIT!

RALPH: Oh *No*!

MANNY: A Wild, Reckless Chase, *Hurtling* though the Darkness.

THOMAS: *Catch* him Max.

MAX: You can count on that.

MANNY: Doreen Hits a Patch of something.

RALPH: ICE!

MANNY: A hundred and fifty miles an hour!

RALPH: Ahhhhh!

MANNY: She Skids, Doreen and the puppy Spinning, Hurtling through the night.

RALPH: *Woa*, Puppy, Hold On!

MANNY: Wham. They land in a ditch. Doreen is shaken. Darkness. Pause.

RALPH: (*To Puppy.*) ...you ok?

MANNY: The cops pull in behind her [Here we go, this is the part] They get out of the car. They trudge toward Doreen across a frozen field.

THOMAS: (*Indicating his flashlight.*) First we turn these on, probably.

MANNY: Yes, good: They flick their flashlights on.

THOMAS: (*Referring to his flashlight, asking everyone.*) [Can I keep this, after?]

RALPH: Can you *What?*

MAX: Stay in it, Thomas.

THOMAS: [sorry.]

MANNY: The Cops [*Focus, Please*] The Cops Approach the Car from Either Side.

THOMAS: (*Miming a knock on the window.*) Knock knock.

MANNY: They rap lightly on the window.

THOMAS: (*A correction.*) Rap.

MANNY: Doreen leans over, rolls down the window, The Bleeding Puppy in her lap. [Good, let's see what happens now.]

*RALPH pulls a mock pistol from a hidden place within his clothing. It has been carefully carved from a soap cake, but is not totally convincing.*

RALPH: Don't Move!

THOMAS: [Hey, what's that one?]

MANNY: It's a Gun!

THOMAS: [Can I look at that?]

MANNY: [Stay in the *Scene*, please.]

RALPH: (*To THOMAS.*) Don't move!

THOMAS: (*To MAX.*) [It looks like Soap.]

RALPH: (*Breaking.*) Oh for crying out loud. See, Manny? I told you.

MANNY: (*To the cast.*) [Hold, please.] (*To THOMAS.*) Thomas?

THOMAS: Yes?

MANNY: It's a *gun.*

THOMAS: It's *shaped* like a gun.

MANNY: No Thomas, it *is* a *Gun.*

THOMAS: [It's soap Max, I'm pretty sure.]

MAX: (*To MANNY.*) Looks to us like soap.

MANNY: We *Pretend* [*Please*] We *Pretend* it's a *Gun.* We *Act* as if it were a *Gun.* Even though we *know* it's Soap, We see that it's SOAP, We ASSUME, for these purposes, That It's A GUN.

THOMAS: (*To MAX.*) [I was surprised he pointed soap at me.]

MAX: [I woulda had the same reaction.]

THOMAS: [You could *clean* something, maybe.]

MANNY: It's a GUN.

THOMAS: [I thought of actually of cleaning something, was my first actual thought.]

MANNY: It's A GUN. The SOAP is a GUN. An actual WEAPON. If Ralph Points the SOAP, He is POINTING a GUN, CAN WE WORK WITH THAT?

MAX: (*To MANNY.*) Easy there, chief.

RALPH: Can't we stop doing this now?

MAX: Let's all try and keep our heads here.

MANNY: Can we get through this one time? Now that we have an *Understanding?* Can we take it from the top?

THOMAS: I'd like to try it again, Max.

MAX: You sure?

THOMAS: Sure. The soap's a gun.

MAX: Alright. From the top.

MANNY: [Thank you.] The Scene, Alright? Speeding, Hurt Puppy, Sirens, Ice, Cops Approach the Car, Flashlights, Here we go. Rap, rap.

THOMAS: (*Miming the knock.*) Rap.

RALPH: (*Directly, to THOMAS.*) What the hell do *you* want?

*Pause.*

MANNY: [Tell Doreen what you *want*, guys.]

THOMAS: You were speeding.

RALPH: So?

THOMAS: …so no speeding.

RALPH: (*Looking at THOMAS.*) What the hell are you *Doing* here?

MANNY: [Tell him what you're doing here, Thomas.]

THOMAS: No speeding.

RALPH: Shut up.

*Pause. MAX and THOMAS look at each other.*

MANNY: Thomas *DO* Something. [Shut *up*, he said.] *Max.*

*Pause.*

You've *Got* to *Do* Something Come *On* Fellas, he's doing a Hundred and *Fifty*, an Insane Person, Endangering Civilians, your *Families.*

THOMAS: [Is the puppy crying?]

MANNY: The puppy is *Screeching.*

RALPH: (*To MAX, abruptly.*) Why don't you just go Home and leave us *Alone*?

MANNY: Doreen is *Assaulting* you Max, *Do* something.

MAX: (*To MANNY.*) I'm a cop?

MANNY: This *Lunatic,* a Bleeding Dog in her Lap, What Do You *Do*?

MAX: I guess probably this.

*MAX reaches into the imaginary car and takes the dog sculpture from RALPH's lap. He drops it to the ground and crushes it casually with his boot.*

RALPH: What are you *Doing*? Manny, he crushed my sculpture!

MANNY: Stay *In* it, Ralph.

RALPH: He crushed my *dog.*

MANNY: He *Killed* it, Ralph. He *Killed* your *Dog.*

RALPH: No, really, This guy's *Crazy.*

MANNY: *Yes,* he's a Sociopath, and He *Killed* the Puppy!

RALPH: (*To MAX.*) What the hell did you do *That* for?

MAX: (*To RALPH.*) License and registration.

RALPH: That was My *Dog.*

MAX: Get outta de cah.

*RALPH draws his soap pistol suddenly from a hidden place within his clothing. He points it at MAX, as if to fire.*

THOMAS: WATCH OUT MAX!

*THOMAS pulls a large, real pistol from a hidden place within his clothing. He points it at RALPH, as if to fire. MAX lunges forward and pushes the gun toward the ceiling. THOMAS pulls the trigger. Bang. RALPH falls to the floor. He puts his hands over his ears.*

MANNY: [Woa, Mama!]

MAX: (*To THOMAS.*) Dammitt, What Did I Tell You?

THOMAS: He *moved.*

*MAX grabs THOMAS and slaps him across the face. Sharply. THOMAS falls to his knees.*

MANNY: (*Regarding MAX, with awe.*) [Holy *Jesus Look* at this guy.]

RALPH: (*Crawling toward MANNY.*) Manny they tried to shoot me.

MAX: (*To THOMAS.*) That is Not the way we behave.

THOMAS: I'm sorry. Jeez.

MANNY: (*Moving toward MAX, away from RALPH.*) [He's *Relentless.*]

RALPH: Manny, that guy tried to actually *shoot* me.

MANNY: *Max.*

MAX: (*Standing over the kneeling THOMAS.*) yeah?

MANNY: I Am In *Awe.*

RALPH: Oh No Manny What are you *doing?*

MANNY: *Look* at you.

MAX: (*To MANNY.*) What.

MANNY: Christ, You're *Emanating.*

MAX: (*To MANNY.*) Really?

MANNY: Are you *Kidding*? Write it *Down*!

RALPH: Oh Manny, please.

MAX: (*To MANNY.*) You think so?

MANNY: *Max.* That's the Scene!

> *Lights.*

## Scene 8

*Later, the office. RALPH holds the Gizmo Box in his lap. THOMAS sits near RALPH, watching MAX and MANNY work.* \*

MAX: So, what's next, whattawe got, There's a kid in a room.

MANNY: Dominic.

MAX: He holds a key.

MANNY: Tony wants the key.

MAX: Tony comes to get it.

MANNY: Right, so Tony: Who is he.

MAX: *What* is he.

MANNY: He's *Hot.*

MAX: Yes he is.

MANNY: He's *Cooking.*

---

\* *THOMAS and RALPH are the audience, MAX and MANNY the players. The movie scene should be performed in a defined area, which RALPH will then enter.*

MAX: Very good.

MANNY: He's on *Fire.*

MAX: Even better.

MANNY: [You know what?] He sort of *is* fire, by this point.

MAX: Keep it coming, Manny.

MANNY: The Saving Doreen Thing.

MAX: That started it.

MANNY: The Shot by a *Cop* Thing.

MAX: [Lemme get a pen.]

MANNY: the Goddam *Roger* Thing, [Put him *Out*, Max, Get a *Hose.*]

MAX: (*Searching.*) [Find a fucking *pen* here.]

MANNY: The whole Doing-it-before-even-having-to-*Think-*About-it-ness of the *Roger* thing.

MAX: He's on a roll.

MANNY: He's on a *Tear.*

MAX: [you'd think there'd be a gross of pens in here.]

MANNY: He's on a *Spree* [See what I'm saying?]

MAX: He's on a spree?

MANNY: He's on A Fucking *Rampage*!

MAX: (*Still searching.*) [Ok, what, a *crayon.*]

MANNY: Every *hair* on his *Head* is standing at Attention, every Breath he *takes* Dims the *Lights* in the Room. The Guy in*Hales* and there's a fucking *Brownout.*

MAX: Holy *Shit*, Manny keep it *rolling*.

MANNY: He's an *Avalanche*, Maxie, He's a Flash *Flood*.

MAX: The *Momentum*.

MANNY: He's a Tidal Wave.

MAX: *Watch* Out.

MANNY: He's a fucking Bandolero, Max, He's a Conquistador.

MAX: Hide the Women and Children.

MANNY: He takes a *Step*, you feel the Tremor, He makes up his *mind* and it is *Fate*, Consider it *Done*. This Guy Has a DESIRE and it is *His*, Do not step in his path, If He Wants a *Key* Dammitt He will HAVE THAT KEY.

   *Pause.*

MAX: I gotta say, Manny, who am I even talking to at this point.

MANNY: really?

MAX: and trust me, I am not given to false praise.

MANNY: You think that works?

MAX: I'll say this. This is what I will say: Clean off the Mantle.

MANNY: (*Modestly.*) Oh come on.

MAX: Clean off the *Mantle* Manny *Make* Room.

MANNY: You think so?

MAX: Get the plaque En*graved* [Jesus Christ, Do I *think* so?] 'M' little 'c' big '*C*.'

MANNY: come on.

MAX: Christ Manny Rent a *Tuxedo* Dammitt Throw *Out* the Bowling Trophy.

RALPH: Hey Manny?

MANNY: [How'd you know I had a bowling trophy?]

MAX: (*Crossing to the Playing Area.*) What happens *Next* Manny, let's take a *look*!

RALPH: Manny?

MANNY: (*Beat.*) Ralph. Yes.

RALPH: (*Beat.*) Hi.

MANNY: (*Beat.*) Is there something you want? (*Beat.*) We're working here, ok?

RALPH: (*Offering MANNY an object from the Gizmo box.*) This is Doreen's diary.

MANNY: Is that relevant?

RALPH: Do you want to look?

MAX: Manny? Let's get to it.

MANNY: (*Turning to MAX.*) Right. [I think he must be dehydrated, little under the weather.] Ok, where are we. I'm Tony. Boom.

MAX: I'm Dominic. I'm a patsy.

RALPH: (*Reading to MANNY, from the diary.*) 'There's two kinds of orphans in this world: Happy and unhappy.'

THOMAS: (*Sotto.*) [You better be careful, Ralph.]

MAX: So what happens next.

MANNY: You're a child, you have a key. I'm insane, I come to take it.

MAX: It's that simple.

RALPH: (*To MANNY.*) Her penmanship, remember Manny? You said Wow she must be some kind of an armless lefty.

THOMAS: [Quiet, Ralph.]

RALPH: Hey Manny?

MAX: (*To RALPH and THOMAS, with startling force.*) If EITHER of you makes a SOUND, I give you my Word, you will not *Ever* make Another. [What. Someone kicked over your *Blocks*?] If I hear you *inhale* you will not have a chance to complete the thought, is that Clear?

MANNY: (*Stepping in between MAX and RALPH.*) The scene Max.

MAX: (*To MANNY.*) I would prefer not to get dramatic.

THOMAS: (*To RALPH, sotto.*) [You gotta try to be *quiet.*]

MANNY: There are distractions. Max? You rise above.

RALPH: This is her locket.

MANNY: (*Leading MAX away from RALPH, toward the Playing Area.*) What's the writer do when the going gets tough? He works on the next part.

MAX: It's distracting.

MANNY: Yes it is. You persevere. The *Scene.* What happens next.

MAX: Alright. I'm Dominic. I'm eleven. I have a key.

MANNY: I'm Tony. I'm coming to get it.

MAX: We begin.

MANNY: Out in the Hall. A Rumbling. An Ominousness. A quaky shaking in floor.

MAX: (*As Dominic.*) 'What's that sound?'

MANNY: Up through your shoes, Up into your *knees.* The pit of your stomach, the Vibration.

MAX: 'What the hell *is* that?'

MANNY: A Glass Falls off a Shelf.

MAX: Smash.

MANNY: Crash.

MAX: The hair stands up on the back of my neck.

MANNY: The door *Rattles* in its frame.

MAX: An Unnamed *Terror* Grips me by the *Throat.*

MANNY: There's a Thumping.

MAX: (*Calling off.*) 'Who's *out* there?'

MANNY: A Humping. A Raging *Is*ness just outside the door.

MAX: I pray to a higher power.

MANNY: The knob turns.

MAX: My hair *Bursts* into flame.

MANNY: (*Entering the Playing Area.*) I enter.

   *Beat.*

MAX: [Jesus Manny I think I may actually *soil* myself.]

MANNY: I don't speak.

MAX: [Christ, I just hand the key over.]

MANNY: [I have that kind of Momentum by this point.]

MAX: [The raging isness, I'm scared half out of my *mind.*]

MANNY: [You just hand Tony the key.]

MAX: (*Miming a handoff.*) *Trembling.* [Say this is trembling.]

MANNY: Boom. What. I Walk Out. (*MANNY turns to exit.*)

MAX: Well, first you kill me. (*MANNY stops.*)

    *RALPH stands. Gizmo Box in hand, he crosses to the Playing Area.*

MANNY: Don't I walk out?

MAX: Are you *kidding?*

MANNY: I *kill* you you think? Aren't you *eleven?*

MAX: Either you kill me or I go to the phone.

    *RALPH stands outside the Playing Area, unnoticed.*

THOMAS: (*Sotto.*) [Be careful, Ralph.]

MAX: I'm already *dialing* here Manny.

MANNY: Wouldn't you be too scared?

MAX: (*Miming a phone.*) Dialing: '*Nine.*' [Say it's a rotary.]

MANNY: Or I tie you up, maybe.

MAX: With who you *are* right now? and you're the Geneva Convention all of a sudden?

MANNY: Well, no, but aren't I very powerful?

MAX: (*Miming it.*) Dialing: 'Nine. One. One.'

MANNY: Hold on a second there.

MAX: (*Into an imaginary phone.*) Hello?

MANNY: (*Pointing an imaginary gun, his forefinger.*) Alright. [This is *nuts.*] Put the phone down.

MAX: (*Into the phone.*) help me.

MANNY: Put it Down!

MAX: (*Into the phone.*) He's got a *Gun!*

MANNY: *Bang.*

*MAX falls to the floor.*

THOMAS: [Dominic falls.]

MAX: …oh my. (*MAX performs death.*)

THOMAS: [Dominic dies. The door opens.]

MANNY: (*To THOMAS.*) It *what?*

THOMAS: [He enters.]

*RALPH takes a step into the Playing Area. He holds the Gizmo Box. MANNY retains the imaginary gun.*

RALPH: I came home.

THOMAS: [A witness.]

MANNY: Woa, wait a *Second,* He is not a witness.

MAX: (*Raising his head, as MAX.*) [Who's this now?]

THOMAS: [It's Ralph. He's a witness.]

RALPH: (*To MANNY.*) I came home.

MAX: (*Standing, intrigued.*) Will you look at *this.*

RALPH: I wanted to ask you something.

MAX: A *Witness* [Good Christ Manny *Now* what.]

MANNY: Now Nothing, this isn't what's happening.

MAX: (*To MANNY.*) You just shot Dominic.

MANNY: Oh please.

MAX: And *Ralph* walks in. [This is Un*believable*] You got the Smoking *Gun* in your hand.

MANNY: No I don't. Ralph, please, stop messing around.

RALPH: Hey Manny?

THOMAS: (*To RALPH.*) How do you know his name?

MAX: Do you *know* this man Ralph?

*Beat.*

RALPH: He was my father.

*Beat.*

MAX: Oh Man we are into some *shit* now. There is a *Witness* [Who appears to be an *Offspring*] –

MANNY: (*To MAX.*) Can you give us one second here please?

MAX: Your *Son, Jesus, Imagine* that Manny, What that must *Feel* like –

MANNY: Yeah, Max, I *understand* –

MAX: A Prodigal Eye *Witness* and there You are with the Smoking *Gun* –

MANNY: (*To MAX.*) You know what might be helpful?

MAX: And *Ralph* shows up, [*Look* at him] In *Diapers* –

MANNY: (*To MAX.*) Is you Not Talking Anymore, That Might Be *Best.* We Got it. Thank You. You not *Speaking* might actually be *Best,* OK Max? Why don't we GIVE THAT A TRY.

*Pause.*

MAX: [fine by me, chief.]

THOMAS: [oh boy.]

RALPH: Manny. I came home.

MANNY: Ralph? you are gonna be the death of me one of these days I swear to God.

RALPH: (*Offering a chair to MANNY.*) Here you go.

MANNY: (*Sitting wearily.*) [You're a good boy Ralph, but you make a person crazy.]

RALPH: Can I ask you a question?

MANNY: I'm sorry if I shot Dominic, that was a mistake.

RALPH: Didn't you used to Love me?

*Beat.*

MANNY: Oh now what are we gonna do here.

RALPH: Did I do something *wrong*?

MANNY: Jesus Ralph, I'm just trying to finish it up.

RALPH: I promise to be good, Ok?

MANNY: That's not what this is about.

RALPH: Oh Manny I hafta tell you I really don't want to be Alone again, I was really getting *used* to us, that whole part, when we were together? I *loved* that part –

MANNY: please.

RALPH: Can we go back to the part when our hearts are a Chorus?

*Pause.*

Please, Manny I don't know what you *want*. Don't leave me alone in here. please. Come back to me.

MANNY: …and then what.

*Pause.*

then what. What would I do? Come play on the floor? [I'd like to, believe me.]

RALPH: So come on then.

MANNY: I can't.

RALPH: *Why?*

MANNY: Because look at me. Is there no Limit? (*Beat.*) [I'm sorry] But do you know what I am? I'm a cesspool. I'm a latrine. They see me coming? They're thinking up new ways to make me eat their shit. (*Beat.*) I have a chance now, Ralph. A chance to Stand Up one time, one time and *Breathe* a little. All I want is a Lungful. Manny McCain. One time, without Shame: Manny McCain.

*Pause.*

MAX: (*To MANNY.*) So what does he do?

MANNY: I'm gonna turn it in, Ralph.

RALPH: oh God.

MANNY: I'm gonna finish it up, I'm gonna turn it in.

*Beat.*

RALPH: (*To himself.*) [and then: here I am, again.]

THOMAS: [Manny stands.]

MAX: [Key in hand, he goes.]

RALPH: Hey Manny?

MANNY: (*Stopping.*) yeah?

> *RALPH reaches into his pocket. He withdraws the portrait of Doreen.*

RALPH: Here. (*Offering the portrait.*) It's no good without this part.

MANNY: Oh Ralph.

RALPH: Be nice to her, Ok?

> *Pause. MANNY accepts the portrait.*

MANNY: …thank you.

RALPH: Goodbye Manny.

> *MANNY exits the Playing Area.*

MAX: (*As if it were a scene.*) Very nice.

> *MAX lifts the silent phone from the desk. He carries it to MANNY.*

> Manny.

MANNY: What.

MAX: Phone for you.

> *Then the phone rings. MANNY lifts the receiver. MAX holds the body of the phone while MANNY talks.*

MANNY: (*Into the phone.*) yeah. (*Beat.**) yeah well thank you very much.

> *Lights.*

---

\* *MANNY accepts congratulations from His Bigness.*

# Scene 9

*Later, the office.*

*Silence. RALPH, MANNY, MAX and THOMAS each sit alone. They wait. Suddenly, the re-revised script comes flying through the mail slot in the door. It lands in the center of the room. A small yellow note is attached to the cover. They look at it.*

MAX: Manny?

MANNY: yeah, one second.

*Pause. No one moves.*

MAX: Are you getting it?

MANNY: Yes I am. Hold on a second.

MAX: (*Standing.*) You want me to get it? I'll get it.

MANNY: (*Stopping him.*) Max I said I would, I'm going, lemme just breathe some air for a second.

*Pause.*

THOMAS: Did it just move?

*Beat.*

MAX: (*Moving.*) Alright.

MANNY: I'm *getting* it Max, I said I would pick it up, I'm picking it up, I said I would so I will.

THOMAS: [*Oh* boy.]

*MANNY crossing to the script. He picks it up, reads the note.*

MAX: So? Where are we.

*MANNY moves purposefully to the phone. He smashes the receiver into the body of the phone repeatedly, viciously. He then knocks the phone to the floor and kicks it, throws it against the wall. He stomps on the remains. He holds the script throughout. MANNY stands over the remains of the phone, breathing heavily.*

RALPH: …hey Manny?

THOMAS: (*To RALPH. Sotto.*) Why did he do that?

RALPH: (*To MANNY.*) Why did you do that?

MANNY: Ralph? Pack your things.

MAX: What does it say.

MANNY: It doesn't say anything. Ralph, please, pack up your box.

MAX: What Does the Note Say?

MANNY: It doesn't *Pertain* to this *Process.*

MAX: Let me see it.

MANNY: Ralph? We're finished here. Dammitt come on.

MAX: Let me see the note.

MANNY: I SAID IT HAS NO BEARING.

RALPH: (*Standing.*) Manny? I'd like to look at that.

MANNY: Ralph, *please.*

RALPH: (*Approaching MANNY.*) Can I see it? [I think I should be allowed to see it.]

*MANNY extends the script reluctantly to RALPH. RALPH takes the script. RALPH reads the note.*

This is hard to make out exactly what this says here. I'm a little on the blurry side. (*Beat.*) Hey Thomas?

*RALPH offers the script to THOMAS, who takes it, then reads the note.*

MANNY: It's al*right*, Ralph.

THOMAS: It says 'yes.'

RALPH: It does? ok yeah, I thought that.

THOMAS: It says, 'Yes but Doreen dies.'

*Pause.*

RALPH: oh. oh. ok…so she *what* happens again?

THOMAS: It says she dies.

*RALPH crosses to a chair, he lowers himself slowly, but misses the chair. He falls to the floor, sits, then lies down on his side.*

RALPH: It's hard to know [I'm just going to lie down for a second] it's hard to tell what's happening.

MANNY: (*Tending to him.*) Ralph, It's Ok.

RALPH: …i'm just lying here for a second, I don't mind.

MANNY: It's alright. It's over now. (*To MAX.*) [OPEN THAT DOOR!]

RALPH: She dies in the end?

MANNY: No.

RALPH: I thought she did, now. Doesn't it say she does now?

MANNY: (*To RALPH.*) Listen to me. We're done. We have delivered. The Script is Complete.

MAX: (*Having taken the script from THOMAS, he now refers to the note.*) That's not what it say here.

MANNY: (*To MAX.*) [YOU OPEN THAT FUCKING DOOR!] (*To RALPH.*) Just stand up Ralph, we can get going.

MAX: Manny?

MANNY: I said THE SCRIPT IS *COMPLETE*. I said we are *FINISHED*.

MAX: and I said that's not what it says here.

MANNY: (*Standing, to MAX.*) Who *are* you?

MAX: What. There's a difference of *Opinion*?

MANNY: You know Nothing.

MAX: Please. You have a *Preference*? Are you out of you *Mind*? You would throw it away [Your *Life*, Manny, all you have done] You Throw It Away, to what. To Please A Child? Look at him.

MANNY: That's *Enough*.

MAX: *Grow* up. It's a Change. An Alteration. She Dies. Manny, who Gives a damn?

MANNY: I said that is ENOUGH. I HAVE HAD ENOUGH. GODDAMMITT You piece of Garbage. You know *Nothing*. The Script is *Complete*. We have Done Your Bidding and I say this: SHE LIVES.

*Beat.*

THOMAS: (*Eyeing MAX.*) [Be careful everyone.]

MANNY: (*Gently, to RALPH.*) Here, come come, give me your arm.

RALPH: Hey Manny, there you are.

MANNY: You're a little woozy?

RALPH: A little.

THOMAS: [Everyone please be Careful.]

*A phone rings, muffled. MAX moves to the desk, opens a drawer and withdraws a phone identical to the one which MANNY destroyed. He places it on the desk, and lifts the receiver.*

MAX: (*Into the phone.*) yeah. (*Beat.*) Sure. (*He hangs up the phone.*) Manny?

*MANNY turns to face MAX. MAX pulls a gun from within his clothing, points it at MANNY and fires. MANNY's chest explodes in a great shower of blood. He falls to the floor, dead. MAX places his gun on the desk and picks up the script. RALPH stands, looking down at the body.*

THOMAS: [Oh Ralph.]

RALPH: (*RALPH kneels by MANNY and nudges him.*) Manny.

*Pause.*

Manny what happened?

*MAX moves to RALPH. He stands over him, holding the script.*

MAX: Ralph? I would think your choice would be fairly clear.

RALPH: (*To the corpse.*) Ok. Ok kiddo, up and Adam. Let's get the heck out of here.

MAX: We're almost finished.

RALPH: Thomas, could you give me a hand please?

MAX: We will complete the job, Ralph. We need a writer.

RALPH: (*To THOMAS.*) He's bleeding.

MAX: You have a choice.

RALPH: (*Quickly finding and opening an object from the box.*)
Here. Here I know. It's the canister of breath Tony gave
her. Breathe this, Manny. *Please.* Take a little breath of
this.

MAX: Alright that's enough. Stand up.

THOMAS: Max?

*THOMAS has picked up MAX's pistol from the desk. He points
it at MAX.*

MAX: Oh, Thomas.

THOMAS: Stop talking.

MAX: What are you doing?

THOMAS: Leave him alone.

MAX: Come on, Thomas, for godssake, put that down.

THOMAS: I WILL SHOOT YOU MAX I SWEAR TO GOD.

*Pause.*

Ralph. Stand up.

RALPH: I think he might be dead, Thomas.

THOMAS: (*To RALPH.*) Listen. Stand up. [Max if you move a
*muscle* I will shoot you though the *heart.*] Ralph. Get up
and walk out the door.

*THOMAS goes to the door and opens it, his gun pointed all
the while at MAX.*

(*To RALPH.*) Right Now.

*RALPH reaches into MANNY's pocket, withdraws the picture of Doreen.*

Ralph. Walk out the *door*, for gods*sake.*

RALPH: (*To the picture.*) hi. (*Beat.*) oh, a little up and down. (*Beat.*) ok. I think that's a nice idea. (*To MANNY.*) Manny? here. We want you to have it.

*RALPH lays the picture on MANNY's chest.*

THOMAS: Ralph, please. Go.

RALPH: (*To MANNY.*) ...bye.

*RALPH stands. RALPH exits. Pause. Then THOMAS crosses to the corpse, the gun pointed all the while at MAX. THOMAS looks at the picture of Doreen.*

MAX: Thomas?

*Pause. THOMAS gazes at the picture.*

What am I about to say to you.

THOMAS: (*Looking at the picture, in awe.*) ...oh boy.

*THOMAS lowers the gun to his side.*

MAX: Thomas, What am I about to say.

THOMAS: Max? look at this.

*THOMAS hands the picture to MAX.\* MAX takes the picture into his hands. Pause.*

MAX: ...oh my.

*Beat.*

---

\* *The audience never sees this picture, nor should they see a shadow of the image through the back of the paper.*

THOMAS: …it's Doreen.

*Pause.*

MAX: oh Lord……she's beautiful.

*The End.*